The Washing Mishap

AF583999

Janine Scott
Illustrated by Jon Davis

It was Saturday.
Dad asked Emma and Johnny
to do some jobs around the house.
Emma had to wash the clothes.
Johnny had to wash the dishes.

“Washing dishes is boring,” said Johnny.
“I don’t like washing clothes,” sighed Emma.
Then Emma had an idea.

She went into the garage.
She crashed and banged.
She hammered and clanged.

“My robot can wash the dishes and clothes,” she said. Emma gave her robot a tea towel and a scrubbing brush.

"Get the dirty clothes and wash them in the washing machine," said Emma to the robot.

"Get the dirty dishes and wash them in the kitchen sink," said Johnny to the robot.

Then Emma pushed the start button.

The robot grabbed the dirty clothes from the washing basket.

It put the dirty clothes
into the sink.

In went the shirts.
In went the shorts.
In went the socks.

Swish, swish, swish...

Then the robot got the dirty dishes from the kitchen.

The robot put the dirty dishes into the washing machine.

Around went the cups.
Around went the plates.
Around went the knives and forks.

Smash! Crash! Clink!

Emma and Johnny came running.
"What's that noise?" they shouted.

“It’s the dishwasher!”
said the robot.